Charles Boyle was born in Leed   g
English in the UK and abroad, and now works in publishing.
He lives in London with his wife and twin sons.

CHARLES BOYLE

Paleface

faber and faber
LONDON · BOSTON

First published in 1996
by Faber and Faber Limited
3 Queen Square London WC1N 3AU

Photoset by Wilmaset Ltd, Birkenhead, Wirral
Printed in England by Clays Ltd, St Ives plc

A CIP record for this book
is available from the British Library

IBSN 0–571–17729–8

Some of these poems were first printed in:
*London Magazine, London Review of Books, Poetry
Review, PN Review, Times Literary Supplement.*

2 4 6 8 10 9 7 5 3 1

Contents

Monday 1

The Miracle at Shepherd's Bush 2

Wiseman's Grand Summer Clearance 4

The Year of the Dog 5

Criminal Fraternity 6

Strongbow 8

March Hares
    (i) Underground 9
    (ii) Overtime 10
    (iii) Seepage 11

The Big Idea 12

The Expert 13

Founders' Day 14

Switzerland 15

Serial 17

Species 18

Unicorns 19

Bedtime 20

Familiar 22

A Certain Age 23

Lissom 25

Velcro 26

Tourism 40

In the Middle Atlas 41

Dry Goods 42

1st Floor, Ladies Fashions 43

Figurine 44

Solid Professionals 45

The Interview 46

September 47
The Optometrist 48
Fast Forward 49
Dutch, 17th Century 50
Later the Same Era 51
New Mains, 1864 52
White City 54
Sheds 55

This poor gambler isn't even a noun. He is kind of an adverb.

Stephen Crane, 'The Blue Hotel'

Monday

My life accused me: paleface, it said, I deserve better.
Is this or is this not an advanced post-industrial democracy?

Useless explaining the menopause, or that one child in three
is born below the poverty line.

We sallied down to the leisure centre.
What are these grey bits, it asked, in my seafood salad?

The Miracle at Shepherd's Bush

By late afternoon you are standing at the barriers
around a patch of scorched grass, a piece of white clothing,
one shoe, a kite in a tree. The women with armbands

are saying nothing, only that no one
has been hurt or arrested. There's a faint smell of burning,
a lingering pink over Acton

that seems reluctant to call it a day. The choir
of the Pentecostal Church sings unaccompanied gospel hymns
and slowly you become aware just how many people

you live among are blind or dumb or are crippled
in so many ways. Some kneel and pray or weep, others light
    candles
on a trestle table covered with velvet or dig divots

of grass and soil which they carry off in plastic bags.
Most people are simply curious, they would like the police
or an archbishop to say for sure whether it is one thing

or another, it resembles too closely for comfort a car-boot sale
or minor demonstration against the government – except there
    lacks
any sense of achievement, of having stood up to be counted.

Blessed by some nuns, warned by a man with a thermos
the end of the world is nigh, you walk home past a couple
in a tent making love. Next day it is in the papers

along with a two-years'-old photo of the boy with his mother
in someone's back garden, not smiling. Eye-witnesses
come forward, though you know for a fact at least two of them

were in the Coningham Arms all day. The lucrative role of
    father
is claimed by three. It rains, the paths worn in the green
are trodden to mud, wheelchairs get stuck, you overhear jokes

about virgin births and burning bushes. For a week,
maybe two, there are reported sightings of the mother and boy
from Stranraer, Teignmouth, Berwick-upon-Tweed,

Oslo. You think of the boy waking
to the sound of water, the morning light, his fingers
touching skin all over that must scarcely feel his own.

Wiseman's Grand Summer Clearance

i.m. T.F.

Red brick and roses, over-green lawns, a wisp of smoke
climbing a little in the airless sky,
then losing heart . . . After the cremation
I walked down to the high street
and stood for a long time
in front of a menswear shop: trousers,
suits and ties, three-packs of handkerchiefs,
shirts with stripes and with button-down collars –
perfectly ordinary decent clothes
that nobody wanted, not even at knock-down prices,
that seemed fated never once to be worn.

banality

The Year of the Dog

Bank managers, bombs in Oxford Street, buying a suit:
it was the year of starting to get serious.
Of letters of application, apology and condolence.
Of a girl sitting cross-legged on the floor
saying she would commit suicide
if she wasn't married by her twenty-fifth birthday –
she just wanted that boy-girl stuff out of the way
so she could concentrate on what was important.
Of playing for time, while admitting
that two copies of *Memories, Dreams, Reflections* in one room
were more than enough. Of knowing something
had to give, but what or who and when? One Friday
I woke up in Notting Hill with yellow greasepaint on my face:
I remember looking down from a tower-block balcony
on an empty playground and thinking it was already too late
to become a surgeon. And when the ageing whippet
I didn't even like
that belonged to the house I was house-sitting
ran off in the park, I felt my life
would never be whole again. I posted a hundred notices
on trees, railings, in local newsagents
offering a £5 reward, a lot of money then.

Criminal Fraternity

the smile of one who is habitually serious
                                        Stendhal

Thinking of that legendary era
when men were men
and women dogs
I recall a night ill spent
in the back of Sonny Leung's.

The Moose shuffled and dealt.
When the one with cannonball hands
reached for his cards
a fuzzy blue angel
slid down his arm.

The one in a natty suit
kept mixing up spades and clubs.
It was enough to make the blood
start weeping from Sonny's scar.
I was treated like one of the gang

but for years afterwards
whatever went wrong in my life
I connected with the albino boy
who came in with a bottle and glasses
and whispered in the Moose's ear.

*

It must have been long past ten,
time for cocoa and bed,
when we lay the cannonball down
on a leatherette settee
and peeled off his blistery lips.

Sonny unplugged his teeth
and counted them into his pocket:
one for each day of October
plus an extra that bounced on the lino
and got crushed by the Moose's boot.

The angel flinched once,
then relaxed. There was something
almost holy –
I found myself thinking
of *The Supper at Emmaus* –

the way the natty one picked his nose,
then held his finger up
as we stood around in silence
like a Quaker congregation
waiting for the spirit to move us.

Strongbow

*I saw no wild or independent Indian . . . but now and again at
way-stations, a husband and wife and a few children, disgracefully
dressed out with the sweepings of civilisation, came forth and
stared upon the emigrants.*

R. L. Stevenson, *The Amateur Emigrant*

Two hours by Intercity north of London
I recall for no good reason
the cider-wrecked hobo

who waved me off, or away . . . And another
of his tribe, a whiskery ex-army tramp
who one dark and stormy night

drank my place dry, tried to clamber
into my bed, then broke down weeping
over a grimy letter –

its business logo, a closed portcullis –
from Enoch Powell, to whom he'd written applauding
the speech about rivers of blood.

Flatlands: thorny fields, ditches being dredged,
a woman out walking her dog . . .
The cooling towers. The burial grounds.

post Larkinesque
corror. of Brit.

March Hares

(i) *Underground*

A woman sleeping on the underground:
neat, Asiatic, fluent in four languages, her finger
still marking the place

in *Islamic History*
by M. A. Shaban: 'By the time 'Umar was suddenly
assassinated he was painfully aware

of the problems of the empire and his impotence
to solve them.' It is 10.17 a.m. –
she has never been

a morning person – and the train is passing
under Chase Manhattan, the Banque de L'Orient Arabe,
the Bank of Yokohama, tunnelling out

to Leytonstone: a ragtag
buffeted place, windy with gusts
of up to 40 miles per hour, a boy

urban
detail/data/
objects/
people

in a shoe-repair shop that also copies keys
who'll briefly imagine her naked,
early blossom on the plane trees.

(ii) *Overtime*

Convalescent, mooching indoors, all day
in the corner of my eye
a dithering on fences, a fear and trembling –

spoilers, scatterbrains, eastern starvelings
blown on a whim
to our avenues and gardens, their call

a cursory trill . . . Lights blaze
through a spindrift rain, the temporary lights
of men working into darkness

on the new development, men on good money
in spartan rooms
hammering and wiring and sanding down

to a dustless sheen; strangers walk by
maybe five minutes sooner or later, no more,
than their usual time

from the bus, coming home: as if this were some daily police
reconstruction, as if a witness's memory
might be jogged into total recall.

(iii) *Seepage*

A monument erected out of public funds
on some grassy knoll
that spoils the view, then becomes the view –

couples marry there, or used to; picnics are held,
rallies, protest marches; people leave bequests
or abseil down it

illegally. Dogs
and the wind favour it; deadlines
slip by, monographs on the New Brutalism

are published and remaindered. It weathers,
darkens, until the ache in its bones
becomes its bones and, reminded of it, people tend to recall

a certain era: gentility, discretion,
piano lessons . . . Tourists flock
to puzzle over the unlikely slogans

that are sprayed around its base, then stand well back
and adjust the focus: that shape behind us
smiling awkwardly, I mean us smiling.

The Big Idea

We were working out our redundancy notices.
We talked on the phone all morning,
looted the stationery, sat around in the canteen
thinking of ways to get rich quick:
maybe write a bestseller, maybe window cleaning
— all you needed was a bucket and ladder,
low capital investment. We emptied our desk drawers
— was this it? the sum total? — and when fire-engines
got snarled in the traffic we stood at the windows
and cheered. It was like the end of term
or the decline of the West, what we'd hardly dared
dream of seemed suddenly possible. Like Susie,
who planned to spend her pay-off on a one-way ticket
to China. She had purple lipstick
and a penthouse flat. She could hold her breath longer
than anyone I've known. We were completely
unsuited, but for the time in question love
was a thing I almost believed could filter through
to the junk yards, the scams, the base-line
of the national economy.

econ.
decline.

The Expert

An old girlfriend appears on TV
answering questions about the homeless.
Yes, the new government initiative
is welcome as far as it goes.
No, it doesn't even attempt
to tackle the root of the problem.

Phones are ringing behind her,
colleagues are bent over keyboards . . .
I want to ask how much she earns,
whether she still leaves the cap off the toothpaste
and if she has children, what are their names?

Just before we go off the air
she gives me that patient look –
as if a grasp of the basic issues
will for ever elude me,
as if I think I can make a difference
by giving money to beggars in the street
or offering them a bed for the night.

complicity ...
private lives | public virtues

indifference world ...

Founders' Day

Recitals. Prizes. Guest appearances
by TV personalities. The ball game
in the park – we lost this year, but the match
had its moments . . .
                              Crowds are drifting home
along Balmoral Avenue, ice-creams,
beer, illegal substances are being consumed,
policemen's arms round happy revellers
for the cameras. I keep recognizing workmates
at the second take, they look different
in jeans or shorts, their faces reddened
from a day of sun and wind, they have wives or girls
they introduce. Kids on blades
zip by, all poise and sway, there's grace in that;
children get bored or pretend to shoot
the silver airship down, circling slowly overhead
with the company logo. There's a shouting man
at the memorial, he just stands beside it
screaming blue abuse at women, foreigners, priests,
the bosses, the workers, humanity in general
– regular, annual, collar and tie,
as if he's paid to do it, this is his job.

People stop around him, admire, applaud,
buy postcards. So much bile
and pain: it could be real, or it could be art.

Switzerland

Today, as it happens, there is no enemy.
John McPhee, *The Swiss Army*

Congratulations on the new job. Helen
must be pleased, not to say relieved. Weekend use
of the company plane? Don't answer. I picture you
in one of those downtown phallic high-rises
on the postcard you sent a while back, all shiny steel
and neutral carpets, a discreet little *ping*
as you arrive on the fortieth floor, the corridors awash
with single women – and you only have to glance
at the keyboard for the national economies of half of Asia
to get the jitters (chaos theory). Then –
I can't help it – something happens, a murder, a cover-up,
a massive fraud that speaks doom to the West
as we know it. Enter the FBI. You've been framed
of course, and only the dogged devotion of this slim dark
patriotic girl in accounts can save you now . . .
The whole thing lasts approximately ninety minutes,
is beautiful to look at, includes a bondage scene
that's genuinely funny, and if you tap it, say,
you'd hear the sound of loose debris
falling down inside – intentional, I know . . . Jane
sends her love. She gets depressed. She goes shopping
in the sales, buys six pairs of boots that neither fit
nor make her look good, then feels too ashamed
to take them back. They're stacked in the bedroom
like heirlooms we can't get rid of. She says the reason
I never ask if she loves me is in case she says yes.
I don't deny it. I'm fond of her as always, never more

than when she comes back muddy and starry-eyed
from her weekend retreats, but this time
the rewind button's stuck, I think we're both in need
of a get-out clause. The weather should but doesn't help:
for weeks it's been so crisp and cold, the sky
so unbearably blue, I feel I'm living in a landlocked
neutral country where uniforms and casual wear
hang side by side in heavy wardrobes carved with griffins,
airstrips scar the forests – like someone's stuck down
Band-Aids, then peeled them off – and the mountains
are stuffed with a kind of bread that keeps for years:
a constant state of readiness for what never happens,
plus a low-level fear that the thing itself
might be mistaken for a routine practice. Altitude
sickness? Post-industrial anaemia? Do you remember that man
who used to knock on the door with his clipboard
petition, reeking of something, a kind of *ancien régime*
aftershave? Save the whales, library opening hours,
political prisoners, sleeping policemen
to cut the through traffic – I signed for everything
but in the end I got tired of playing good neighbours
and gave him the number of Madame Lynne – who for £25
tells me I can have everything I want
if I just *allow it to happen*. I haven't seen him since.

Serial

The things I did to Susie
and other such episodes –

like the demented pacing
of the mature student upstairs,

still struggling with his thesis
on the death of the author,

or the unfunny catchlines
of retired comedians

wheeled back on stage
for *This is Your Life*.

Species

When you look at me as if to say
That's the first meaningful thing you've said in months
I immediately want to take it all back
into a small purse, and let someone else pay.

I want to get drunker than I was last April
and not to be bothered to do all the things I suddenly know
I can do without trying.
I want to hand in my notice.
I want to sit in the kitchen wearing my trusty blue shirt
and read *Parade's End* from page 1 to page 906
without answering the phone, the door or the call of nature.
I want to go back twenty years to a Friday night in the Café
   Amphitryon
and start my life again from there
and be stubborn enough to repeat it all exactly
down to the last visit to the fucking launderette.

I want to stand with you in front of an endangered species –
200 in the president-for-life's reserve, then sixty,
the single final innocent misfit
comatose in its sleeping quarters or scraping its flank
against the bars, a sad disappointment
after the vivid illustrations in the books for children –
and see where that gets us.

imposs.
wants

[18]

Unicorns

A sort of dusty white, with stubby horns
that leave scaly flakes on your hands –
between the goats and donkeys
in the children's section
they are chomping their vitamin pellets.

There's a map of the world
with a few red dots, plus a text explaining
their shrinking habitat.
They don't look in danger, just tired,
or restless . . . And though of course

they should be returned to the wild
and set free, they appear to lack
whatever it takes, so on balance we agree
that their being where they are
is probably the right thing.

Bedtime

holes in the sky
little monkeys peek
through the eastern gate
the street of weavers
tinsmiths alley

old woman mad as the wind
hairy scary
chasing a chicken
blood when it spills
fire-engine red

in the vizier's palace
soldiers in shakos
don't blink don't speak don't hear
people vanish
in front of their bony noses

walls have ears tables groan
heads roll
men with long white beards debate monotheism
in seven languages
no one waters the plants

will the prince on his steed
arrive in time rescue the princess
die in his bed
now the children are sleepy
they've seen enough

the knife grinder the accordion man
the night watchman with lumps on his head
bears dancing
the seller of jujubes
the chicken up and running

Familiar

(i)

Watch out for the sheep! I want to tell them,
my children the size
of two people seen a mile away
climbing steadily above the treeline.
I mean the wolves pretending to be sheep.

(ii)

A man with two heads, we saw him.
A woman dressed as a bear.
Fire engines, the storybook kind they put out to grass.
A band of Red Indians drinking takeaway teas
on a lorry decked out with Christmas tinsel.
Some cowboys, some medieval knights in plastic armour
rattling buckets. Spotty-faced boys in blue
with trumpets and drums, all-American girls in tutus
feeling the cold. It was early
on New Year's Day, the sky was grey, fretful,
it began to sleet, then this man with his patch
of coloured – no, it was the flag
of the motherland
and fatherland.

A Certain Age

At evening supper, the father is eaten up by the children.
Louise Bourgeois

The men soldier on, treading water.
They keep leaving the garden gate unlocked.
They dream of their winning shots through the covers
for the under-16s, wake with a familiar sour taste in their mouths
that reminds them of their fathers, and in summer
they train their eyes not to linger
on their neighbours' teenage daughters' legs
by calling to mind their own.

The women cry easily.
Having forgotten what it was they wanted
they will stop suddenly in the middle of the street
causing two-mile tailbacks. Later they remember
and wonder why it seemed so urgent. On Tuesday afternoons
I accompany them in spirit
as they drive out to the gravel pits
to watch the rain.

Girls from war-torn countries who smoke in the park
are just one of our badges of guilt.
Sometimes a great wind blows in from the east
and we huddle together feeling poor and bare and forked.
Next day he's still there, like the government,
like life as it needn't be but is,
the hairy muttering man at the end of the road
clutching the noise of his own brain to his one good ear.

Tired, late, after the waiters have all gone home,
we stare into each other's eyes until one of us
is forced to look away. Truancy haunts us –
people who simply vanish, or the story of the mine-worker
who, rounding the shoulder of the mountain,
saw an avalanche had buried all his mates.
The whole landscape held its breath.
He had no second thoughts.

Bright, handsome and devouring children,
already older than we think, may be all we have.
We watch them curiously, helplessly, like exotic animals.
We teach them our bad habits.
When they go into hospital we sit outside swing doors
reading free magazines
while waiting for the nurse to come out and tell us the worst,
it's her job to do this.

No one asks us what our hobbies are, people don't
as a rule ask questions. Our secret wishes?
Our biggest mistakes? Our sorrows, consolations, distinguishing
features? When strangers to these parts
look at me twice, thinking they know me,
thinking I'm 'Roger', friends, I say, Romans, I'm a man,
I've been around if not far, I can hum a few tunes,
my patience is finite, I swing my arms as I walk.

Lissom

I'm sitting alone in a room
with a bandage round my head
doing nothing wrong.

Two or three times a day
a girl in her early twenties
holding a Mongol bow

comes to the open door
and looks briefly around
for the arrow.

Velcro

mark anthropology
[anthropological poet]

Renous, alluding to myself, asked him what he thought of the King of England sending out a collector to their country, to pick up lizards and beetles, and to break stones? The old gentleman thought seriously for some time, and then said . . . 'I do not like it: if one of us were to go and do such things in England, do you not think the King of England would very soon send us out of the country?'

Darwin, *Voyage of the Beagle*

There's a tribe, I swear it,
in the Syrian desert
who bury their dead standing up.

Every five years, a great sandstorm
rages; diviners interpret
the chattering of skulls.

*

Their warrior queen
models Armani. Their children
are force-fed videos

of the long march
out of Crittenden
to Zit. Their god is named

after the terrifying noise
made by the opening
of a hundred tent-flaps at dawn.

*

The acrid leaves they chew
every waking hour
produce a mild

hallucinatory effect
of the kind experienced
by publishers' reps

while driving on the M6
north of Carlisle
in light drizzle.

*

Because their topography
lacks high places
they have yet to invent

the ladder. Because
of the premium they place
on originality in art

no two toothbrushes, funeral masks
or wheels
are exactly the same.

*

While their diligent wives
are putting on their faces
the junior elders

assemble in the lobby
to smoke cheroots
and discuss the pros and cons

of the new technology –
franking machines, ejector seats –
over laced mint tea.

*

Lobbies, vestibules, the paths
or no man's land
between clan enclosures –

'zones of the veil'
in which a code of anonymity
is *de rigueur*,

in which nevertheless
certain covert proposals
are frequently advanced.

*

Sex: *see under* alabaster;
Earhart, Amelia; Friday.
See also tongs.

It's not that they don't
enjoy it, but are often inhibited
by their distracting need

to rationalize the gap
between the gritty norm
and their culture's pellucid ideal.

*

The present *fatir* – oracle
of the supreme being,
paraded in public

only once every forty-two years
and in times of extreme
political crisis –

is a copy dating
from the 1950s, the original
having been lost.

*

Travellers are welcome
during the feast of Gordon
but should take care to depart

before the unwonted outpouring
of intertribal affection
is bitterly regretted.

*

Small roadside cairns
mark the graves of children
hit by cars

while dashing out
in playful ambush
of foreign buyers

for beads and lucky charms
laid out in rows
on plastic sheets.

[29]

Dust. Boredom. An ant
buried under a handful of sand
scrabbles and blusters

its way to the surface
only to be buried again . . .
Each year the elders

devise yet more creative
firework displays
and evening classes.

A sinecure for life
is awarded annually
for the most formally elaborate

Horatian ode
that celebrates the virtues
of working women –

their hardiness
and sufferance,
their brazen knees.

The Mawami's pigtails
are unrelated
to the fanciful hairstyles

in the famous mezzotint
of 1821
by Thomas Hobson,

an inveterate liar
who never left
his native Lyme Regis.

*

Renowned abroad
for his charitable works
and stylish dressing,

the Mawami remains
conservative at heart —
rather than hear

bad news, he has the throats
of messengers slit
before they can speak.

*

Their champion athletes'
habitual loping gait —
acquired by years of running

through loose sand —
is much imitated
by both teenage boys

who wish to attract a mate
and girls protesting
at the restraints upon their sex.

[31]

*

The pauses
in the speech of the old –
neither shortness of breath

nor the occlusion
of memory,
but steadfast adherence

to the rules of grammar:
each word being set
in its frame of silence.

*

Lifetimes have been gladly spent
mastering just one
of their sacred texts

by scholars who still confuse
the place names and numbers
that may also serve

as intimate endearments
with those that articulate
disgust.

*

To sons departing
on government scholarships
for study abroad

mothers give pellets
of hardened camel dung
as *memento mori*.

Traces may be found
among the dust and fuzz
in their jacket pockets.

*

Booty carried home:
Levi's, Anglepoise lights,
cordless toasters;

a working knowledge
of alleles, zygotes, ~~fertilized ovum~~
stress fractures

forms of
gifts

and of the sexual preferences
of older women
in South Dakota.

*

Ever since the cataclysmic
civil war
between al-Origbi and Philip

twins have been both shunned
and revered –
for the drear month of penitence

that follows their birth,
for the good times enjoyed
by the priesthood.

[33]

*

No less than the beauty
of their sheltered daughters,
the limpid simplicity

of their myth that accounts
for the birth of the world
compels assent.

*

For that one four goats,
a Sanyo fan
and access rights

to a dubious well.
For this a green card.
And for this true love

plus a room of her own —
no girl
without her brideprice.

*

Twice a day
for seven weeks
in a chipped tin mug

a mixture of earwax,
fertiliser
and the liquor sold

by the blind widow
will guarantee exemption
from military service.

*

Cleaning the filters,
raking the dunes —
the hereditary labour

of the *doowalis*.
Bourgeois standing
is signified

by having nothing pressing to do
and a vacant expression
in the bloodshot eyes.

*

The coincidence
between the combined ages
of the Mawami's wives

and the acquisition number
inked behind the ear
of the hunting fetish

in the museum of folk art
in Aleppo
has been remarked.

*

As also the perfect circles
and figures-of-eight
described by caravans

whose raddled guides
still navigate
by the stars —

the Molars,
the Gang of Four,
the Timid One.

*

From December to March
a seasonal wind
infiltrates sand

into every orifice.
Domestic violence
and hard-core video rentals

peak, lending support
to those who argue
for stricter censorship.

*

The wind itself,
say their opponents,
is to blame.

They attack it with knives,
harpoons; or woo it
with tenderness,

[36]

hanging feathers and chimes
on the boughs of trees
to temper its spirit.

*

Rights are reserved,
liability disclaimed.
Prisoners' last words

are contrite
and pre-recorded.
Their code of justice

roughly translates: a tooth
for a camelhair coat,
an eye for a Toyota.

*

Fish: the food of the devil.
Also, those afflicted
by an unaccountable sadness,

an *ennui*
without rhyme or reason,
a joyless desolation

bordering
on the psychopathic, are said
to be dreaming of fish.

*

Knowing as we do
their temperate habits,
their love of children and animals,

their outstanding contributions
in the field of traditional
music and dance, how can we

give credence
to their alleged involvement
in the events at Wadi Haar?

*

At dusk among the baobab trees
or in broad day,
enchanting you

with their broken English,
les petits voleurs
slipping their fingers

under, between, inside –
who steal your heart,
who clean you out.

*

By night, suddenly,
the Blowman will come.
Directly above the spot

where he will ejaculate
the glorious seed of the ancestors
into the sand,

[38]

a cloud in the shape
of *Phoenix dactylifera*
will mushroom in the sky.

*

Sundown. Cooking smells,
diesel oil. The dunes
a darkening mauve.

A low-flying Mirage
rips the sky in two
along a dotted line –

in one half djinns, fabulous creatures,
in the other the eye
of a desert storm.

*

The cache
of lighter fuel, soda siphons
and stolen cheque books

found in a ditch
by H. du Plessix Smith
is not, as previously supposed,

a bluff, a feint
to put off tomb-robbers,
but the real thing.

Tourism

A sluggish tide, a small surprising wind.
A zigzag iron stairway still too hot to step on.
Ropes, gantries, rust, rats.

Not to mention the rider on his rearing horse
no one has the heart to topple
facing the wrong way, out to sea . . .

The weekly packet, three days late: the old folk
disembarking, their suitcases tied with string,
the young getting on with dayglo backpacks.

The dog, the petrol station, the lemon trees.
The girl — seventeen at a guess — locked
in a backroom, fidgeting with her hair.

mystery.
danger.
threat.

In the Middle Atlas

[handwritten annotation: another travel / adventure (cf. early Auden)]

I wore the same clothes for eight days running,
some nights slept in them, some nights didn't sleep at all.
Like a Greek chorus, the dogs in the villages barked
but kept their distance, a stone's throw.

I talked to fewer and fewer people, but more intense:
a man who was Jesus, a woman who growled.
My own voice
was barely audible, I had to repeat everything twice.

The first hour in the city was like a gatecrashed party –
then a party upstairs or across the street . . .
One morning I counted the girls
I would have paid all the money I had to sleep with,
and in the afternoon the ones I wouldn't.

I climbed the hundred and ninety-nine steps
of the ruined minaret without pausing for breath.
Cars made way, women took their children in hand
so I could land without causing undue damage.

Dry Goods

The dumb Swede is buying canvas.
Mrs Fitzpatrick can't decide between the blue and the pink.
Looking sheepish and old and naked
the sheriff wants a new pin for his badge.

A train, abandoned by its mother, utters a mournful wail.
The Carson brothers have shot nobody dead for a week.
The frontier between good and evil
is defended with linen, bonnets and balls of twine.

Nothing disturbs the noonday quiet
except the snores of Judge O'Halloran
and a scratching under the stairs,
the errand boy playing with matches.

1st Floor, Ladies Fashions

My friends, have you ever seen a large crowd
of wives? It's a painful surprise.
                        Yasunari Kawabata, 'The Rainy Station'

Pearls, twin-sets, pearly music:
a cloud of unknowing,
of being wrapped or tenderly stifled

in something light and expensive that keeps out the cold:
a heady brew
of expectancy and surfeit ˙

and displaced angels, their eyes
flickering, grazing the wares, their hands
touching linen, silk, fur, fleece,

then letting go; their dry mouths, their blood
thinning, their every trespass recorded
on soft-focus video

that speaks of crime, degradation, of art-school art
that 'challenges our assumptions of gender
and normality' . . . Dispersing at last

into a street of November rain
where cars stop-go, stop-go:
the red ones, the black, the yellow, the blue.

[43]

Figurine

painted / sculpted / frozen movent. —

I like too
the shape you make
when you're trying on a new little something,
when facing away
from the full-length mirror
you hollow your back,
make a half-turn
so that the heel of one foot's lifted up,
and look appraisingly down
to observe the effect
from behind —
as if you're following yourself
home
incognito.

Solid Professionals

Their brass plates, walnut, leather-bound
tomes, even
their dry skin, steady hands and shiny cufflinks

have the finish
and rectitude of death – of one
upon another, processional . . . With a clearing

of their throats they summon
or dismiss their quality slave-girls, little peaks
of evolution. They smile

their headmaster's smiles and look out the window
at winter trees that have laid down their arms
and lend me their priceless pens.

They dig deep in their waistcoat pockets and toss coins
high in the air
where they hang like childhood memories

before coming down heads – George V
again, I note,
as they peel on their sterile disposable gloves.

[45]

The Interview

He has sat for too long in a boardroom
hung with giant abstract paintings named after cars
or heroes in Greek mythology, doodles
on the pad on his knee
accreting like an invasive disease.

Clocks above the founder's bust
tell the time in New York, Tokyo and childhood.
Lifts ceaselessly raise and lower
the same cubic feet of rumours and silence.
A pale girl makes tea.

Life is not, the poet says, a walk across a field:
the wind ruffling the grass, a piece of forgotten machinery
rusting at the edge . . . His bullet head,
his house in the suburbs, another man
who's done time at a desk.

v. bohemian
image of
poet —
another desk wallah

September

I was walking in the country
with my third wife, who was also my first
(my second one lives in Holland).
We stopped on a bridge
to watch the water flowing under.

The dry brown ferns, the crisp packets
and empty beer cans
were as utterly familiar
as the feeling of being lost,
of not knowing even the time of day.

Likewise the crying in the undergrowth
of an abandoned child, an infant Moses.
We took turns carrying it   .
over fields and stiles
to a roadside garage, where two red tractors

stood cheek to cheek
on the forecourt, pressure-hosed
and burnished
as squat gods, and a man came out to meet us
shading his eyes and scowling.

The Optometrist

Do very tall buildings
only seem to tilt?
Is it true – *objectively* true –
that the girls with the longest legs
wear the shortest skirts?
Why is it invariably
men in deserts
to whom the godhead appears?

Let's pick a desert,
you and I,
filter it somehow,
fire it to the degree you say,
grind it etcetera
and see what we can see –
angel number 101
break-dancing on your tiepin?

Fast Forward

(ageing/time)

One moment my four-year-old is winding my watch —
'*to make it go faster*' —
and the next I'm sitting with a boy of maybe twenty
in an airport lounge. My right arm
is clamped round my hand-baggage, my left is reaching
for what I hope is a gin-and-tonic
and the bulge in my jacket pocket must be my ticket
and passport, if they bother with those any more.

Dreams and destinations: spills, delays: a face
in the crowd that could be her but isn't . . .
Meanwhile my son is explaining — patiently,
indulgently, even while he knows I haven't a clue —
some process to do with his work: how its details
all add up, its incorruptible logic.

Dutch, 17th Century

At 2 a.m. I go down on my knees to the oven
with a vengeance. I do the top of the skirting boards
and where the round bit curves in; the taps; under the lip
of the WC; and from where the water drains
from the shower I fish with a coathanger the matted slime
of my hair and yours.

I could invent a hinged brush to go round the S-bend.
I could drown the cats
and paint the living room a delicate off-white.
While you go on sleeping, unknowing, an Iron Age hill fort
in the heart of England, I could erase
all traces of human habitation.

Tomorrow you could slam the front door without speaking
and I could sit all day with the answerphone on
pretending I'm not waiting for the sound of your key, back
from the charity shop with your hundred black T-shirts
which you'll heap in the wardrobe exactly as they were
or as near as will make no difference.

Or your stiff brisk sweep of the yard
will wake me, and your little cry
as the woodlice scuttle like ambushed hoplites
and the pink worms squirm. Through the Windowlened
    bathroom window
I'll see you lean on the broom like a burgher's skivvy
out of Pieter de Hoogh, a name I could spit.

Later the Same Era

At weekends
we drive out to the reforested counties
to see the new wolves.
Their breeding has exceeded all forecasts.
We pose with our kill
for photographs we send to our friends
signed with the names of dukes and earls.

The moon
is no longer floodlit. We are covered
against acts of God. Wall-to-wall software
has taken the place of silence, the government,
the weather: a monotone like glass in which everything
is made clear. Hardly anyone remembers a time
when they blushed in embarrassment
or life had a 'meaning'
or windows jammed . . .

Sometimes desire
still keeps us awake during nights
after windless days: the ache itself
of continuous wanting, a wire stretched taut
between two high places. Sometimes that wire is plucked.

New Mains, 1864

How did the horses
get into Rossini? (How did the flavour
of absolute innocence
get into Barletta's confection? Or Barletta himself
into his son's new suit?)

By biting the rope, I'd guess,
that tied the paddock gate. Then cantering up
through Hendry's field to where the town band
were giving their all, elbows and cheeks
and serious faces not missing a beat

as they scattered among us
frisking their tails, nuzzling for sugar.
And stayed, a consecration,
all day, unfazed by the dogs, the children,
the speeches, the getting drunk, the endless,

never-shortening queue
outside the old dairy, its chilly breath
of canvas-wrapped ice – where Barletta's wife
with her great tin spoon is filling our mugs
with the slithery goo.

Which tasted, love, both homespun
and eerie. Of sheets
brought in from the line. Of birds that unfurl
like a black cape above a city square. Of model factories
in wooded valleys, of children shading their eyes

against the silvery flash
of a biplane's wings. Of stainless steel. Stravinsky,
Kandinsky. The Bauhaus. Garden cities. A statue
in the harbour's mouth of Signora Barletta, holding aloft
a gi-normous cornet.

Or the word *forever*
whispered among the holm oaks
after we'd slipped out separately
under the nonchalant gaze of the horses
from the dance in MacMaster's barn.

jottings of
memories stored —
but uncharted
(references which remain
within...)

White City

They will be selling our clothes, I know that now.
Our biscuit tins. Our boxing gloves.
Our rolls of surplus wallpaper.
Our tools and gardening equipment, hammers
and rusted sickles and the rake with bent tines.
Our model soldiers.
Our wireless set, on which we listened
to the national anthem and the racing results from Catterick.
Our loved ones and anniversaries
and twilit landscapes in their rickety frames; our books,
bookshelves, light-bulbs even, our watches
that stopped on our wrists.

They will have laid them all out
in rows or piles on groundsheets or trestle tables
or in the backs of hatchback cars.
It will be early in the morning
on the day of our Lord, the sky too will look blotched,
stained, used and abused, a wind out of it
rapidly losing patience. And not
that we'll need them or care a damn who owns them,
but small chemical reactions
we might another day ignore will make it imperative
we buy them back, haggling a little
until the price is right.

Sheds

The way weeds and stiff grasses have reclaimed the yard,
the way the tracks lead frankly nowhere;
the dry rust, the continuous mockery
of insects, of birds; the way the toolsheds
could still be nothing but toolsheds
even without their tools, with their corners smelling of shame
and their little piles of filth . . .

Exhaustion, waste, relief
at being one again with nature –
and still a kind of reckless belief
that just one more day, another hour of light
would have seen it through.

shed - level of existence
(+ shed as
manifestation
of human hope)
bravovans
against odds i.e. value
futility of
self - delusion ...